Walking with Families through Grief

Patricia M. Robertson

Contents

Introduction

She was the first friend I made after the move from the big city, Flint, Michigan, to the village of Concord, Michigan; the first close female friend I had had for a while. Amidst the daily responsibilities of being a wife, having babies and pastoring a church, I had little time to maintain old friendships, much less establish new ones. As such, Sally had been a gift to me. We clicked immediately in a way I hadn't since my college roommate. It was a situation of having a need fulfilled I hadn't even recognized I had until out of the blue it was filled. Only she had a slow-growing brain tumor that eventually took her life.

At thirty-five, I had never had anyone I was close to die. I had visited a number of church members who had died, but none of them affected me like Sally's death. Though I visited other church members every other week, I found it much harder to visit Sally. It was just too hard, and besides, Sally was my friend. As a friend, she understood if I didn't visit more often, I told myself. And she did. There was never any recrimination or suggestion that I was not visiting enough. She appreciated when I visited, even if only once a month.

At one time she had told me about the experience of being in the hospital after brain surgery, in post-op, and being in excruciating pain. Each time, just as the pain became more than she could handle, she felt herself being lifted up by loving arms, the pain subsiding and a peace she could not explain spreading throughout her body. Then she was placed back on the table until the pain grew unbearable once again.

As she grew weaker, I remembered this story and would envision her being held by loving arms. This image gave me comfort whenever I worried about her over the course of her illness.

I was present when she died. She had been staying with her parents since her daily care had become too much for her husband who also had the care of their two children. She was breathing quietly as I prayed by her side. In another room, I could hear someone crying, saying how they couldn't bear to see her this way. In my mind I saw her once again being held in loving arms, in Jesus' embrace. As I prayed, Jesus stood up with Sally in his arms and began to walk away, as Sally took her last breath. I didn't know what to think or do at this point. It appeared that Sally had been waiting for me before she died – her final gift to me. I realized that her family should be notified and I called them in.

I went away feeling confused and unsure. I had never been at the side of anyone who had died before. Had she actually died, or had I imagined it? Maybe she started breathing again when I left. It was only after I received the call confirming what had happened that I began to slowly accept what I couldn't accept, that she was gone.

It has been over twenty five years since this happened but it remains vivid in my memory. Her death was followed by a wide range of emotion as I grieved her loss. It was an emotional roller coaster: In one minute I would feel joyful, remembering that experience at her death, and the next I would be crying as I tried to make sense of it. There were feelings of abandonment and jealousy because Jesus had taken her and left me. Sweets that I loved, no longer had an appeal to me. I lost around fifteen pounds in the months after her death. Over time, though, I adjusted and went on with my life without my friend, reminding myself that I would see her again someday; when that happened, it would be as if we had never been apart.

Sally's death had hit me hard because she was my age and also because she had been filling an important need in my life, the need for a female friend. The course of grief was hard. In contrast, the grief I experienced after my dad's death was much easier. He had lived a good life and had not experienced an untimely death. His death didn't go against nature – parents are supposed to die before their children. I still miss him, but it wasn't the gut-wrenching loss that Sally's death was.

Another major loss in my life was the death of my first marriage in divorce. This was complicated by years of wondering, would we maybe get back together? Divorce is a death, but there is no dead body to tell you it is over, just a piece of paper. I cried my share of tears over this ending, as well as spent time in counseling in order to come to some resolution and acceptance of the situation.

And most recently was the loss of employment when my position as chaplain at a retirement community was eliminated, followed a year later by the end of my position as Director of Family Ministry at my church, two very different situations eliciting different forms of grief.

In the first, I was taken by surprise when in the space of one hour I went from being gainfully employed to sitting in my car with the contents of my office packed into the trunk and back seat. No time to say goodbye to people I had grown to love over the previous twelve years, no time to prepare. I was left in a state of shock, which gave way to anger and took me more than a year to overcome.

In the second situation, I knew well in advance and was not surprised when given notice that my position was being eliminated. I was given ample time to prepare, tie up loose ends and say goodbye, and it was handled in a manner where I was able to maintain relationships I had at the church, including the one with my pastor, the bearer of the bad news.

Two similar situations yet two very different outcomes.

A Lifetime of Loss and Transition

All of life is change. Some are more pleasant than others; some we look forward to, others we dread. But change happens whether we embrace it or not. It is unavoidable.

Jane had longed for this baby, anticipated its birth for months and was ecstatic that she had arrived into the world with all of the necessary body parts, a healthy baby girl. So why was she so teary-eyed and sad? It wasn't just post-partum depression, or the natural exhaustion from the physical demands of labor and delivery. Much as they had wanted the baby, with every change comes a loss. They had yet to allow themselves to grieve over what they had lost — the freedom to come and go as they please, freedom from the constant demands of caring for a newborn, freedom to focus on themselves. In their joy over their daughter's birth, they were not acknowledging the loss.

With every change we gain and we lose. For those changes we look forward to, graduation from high school or college, marriage, the birth of a baby, a new job, we have a tendency to focus on what we have gained without acknowledging our loss and the grief associated with that loss. Each of these are mini-deaths. For those changes we dread — death of a loved one, the loss of a limb or health, loss of employment, loss of a relationship — we have a tendency to focus only on the loss, the negatives, without acknowledging that hope remains, hope for a new life out of the death of the old.

While we may experience many losses in life, this book will focus on losses due to the death of a loved one, with some mention of other situations. We will explore normal grief versus complicated grief. We will enter into the world of the grieving in order to understand our own reactions and our loved ones' reactions and thereby walk more readily alongside those who are grieving, allowing them the space that they need at times as well as offering support when needed.

This book is for ministers, clergy, lay people, counselors, anyone who has suffered a loss or is helping others through their losses. It is designed to explore some of these different faces of grief and how to walk with others through grief to new life. Their journey is our journey as we travel through this life together.

Chapter 1

Faces of Grief

He couldn't believe she was gone. He was sure he saw his wife at times in a crowded supermarket or walking on the street, just an arm's length away but when he reached for her she was gone. She was just out shopping with her friends, an activity she loved to do. She would be home soon, he told himself, only to face an empty bed at night, an empty seat at the table. Sometimes he was sure he was going crazy as he forgot appointments, found himself wandering on the street, not sure how he got there.

She went to the gravesite every day. She didn't care if others thought she was crazy as she carried on a conversation with her dead child, telling her how much she missed her, filling her in on all of the details of life, sobbing until there were no more tears left.

C.S. Lewis, in his book, *A Grief Observed*, and Madeline L'Engle, in her book, *Two Part Invention*, on her marriage to Hugh Franklin, both write about the loss of their spouses to cancer; however, Lewis was still young in his love for Joy Davidman when she died, having been married for a short time, whereas L'Engle lost her husband after forty years of marriage. Both grieved tremendously, but in different ways, unique to their own personality and their differing situations. That's a reminder to me that the face of grief is as varied as the people involved.

In the introduction I shared five different situations of loss. In each one I experienced grief, however the grief was different, having five different faces. George Engle, in his article, "Is Grief a Disease? A Challenge for Medical Research," (*Psychosomatic Medicine*, 1961) compared the psychological loss of a loved one to the physiological trauma experienced by a burn victim or someone who has been severely wounded. In both cases, healing over time is required and while full function can be restored, some may adapt better to the loss than others.

How a person experiences grief is affected by multiple factors, including their own personality and history of dealing with loss, their relationship with the deceased, and factors around the loss. While there are symptoms of loss that are commonly experienced, each person will experience them to a lessor or greater degree depending on those factors. In this chapter we look at those symptoms, the factors that affect our grief and ways of processing grief.

COMMON SYMPTOMS OF LOSS

The bereaved may feel like they are going crazy at times. This is normal. Life as they knew it has been turned upside-down and they don't know how to proceed with the task of living. They may experience a roller coaster ride of feelings from excessive bouts of crying, to rage, to numbness and shock or relief that their loved one is no longer suffering. These feelings may be like waves of the ocean, threatening to swallow them up. They may feel their loved one's presence or think they see them in a crowd, further cause for them to question their sanity. They yearn for the deceased and keep expecting them to show up despite having seen the dead body being lowered into the grave. They pray that it is all a bad dream that they will wake from some day. Or their loved one may come to them in their dreams.

Many people exhibit behavior changes. Gregarious, people-loving individuals may withdraw from social activity. Others may find themselves absent-minded, forgetting appointments, forgetting where they left their car, to the point of wondering if there was something wrong with them. They may have difficulty sleeping or loss of appetite. Some may throw out any tangible reminder of their loved one, while others treasure objects that belonged to the deceased, carrying them with them at all times or returning repeatedly to the gravesite or places associated with their loved one. All of these can be part of normal grief.

Physical symptoms can include tightness in the chest and throat, hollowness in the stomach, oversensitivity to noise, feeling short of breath, muscle weakness, dry mouth, lack of energy. The bereaved may be exhausted, feeling tired all the time from the hard work of grieving. They may go to sleep then toss and turn all night, leaving them tired all day. Someone who is grieving may be more prone to serious health issues. Within the first year of a major loss, many bereaved experience health decline or a major illness. I always encourage those dealing with loss to attend their yearly physical and take care of themselves, something they rarely feel like doing.

Other times these symptoms cause them to seek out their physician for help. After my father's death, my mother complained about a heaviness in her chest. When she mentioned this to her doctor at a routine visit, her doctor immediately sent her to a heart specialist to be checked out. The heart specialist found no problems. My mom was experiencing the physical manifestations of a broken heart.

These are but some of the wide variety of symptoms related to grief. No one will experience all of these symptoms. It's helpful to be aware of the different symptoms so we can reassure ourselves and our loved ones that what they are experiencing is within the realm of normal, something that those who are grieving have a difficult time recognizing. What is normal, they may ask? Will I ever feel "normal" again?

FACTORS AFFECTING THE GRIEVING PROCESS

Many factors affect the grieving process. Following is a list of the most common ones.

1. Who the person who died was and the nature of the attachment

Was he a beloved spouse, a doting parent, a young child, a sibling, a friend or lover? All impact how you experience their loss. If a parent, was the relationship a close one, or had parent and child been alienated for years? If a child, was it a young child, or an adult child?

In the introduction I mention the deaths of my father and my friend Sally. In the first case, I had had ample time with my dad during the two years before he died as he experienced health issues and hospital stays so that we had no unfinished business. I didn't feel guilty that I had not spent enough time with him and while it hurt to let him go and I still miss him, my grief wasn't as great as with the loss of my friend. Sally had been filling an active need and the fact that she was close to my age brought home to me my own mortality in ways my dad's death didn't. My dad's death was in line with the "natural course of life" — death after a long and fulfilled life, whereas Sally left far too soon.

If someone has an estranged relationship with a parent, they may experience grieving for what they never had and the fact that they no longer have the opportunity to restore the relationship. They may claim they don't feel any loss, only to be surprised by an upsurge of feelings later. Conflicted relationships often lead to complicated grieving which may take longer to resolve.

The death of a casual acquaintance may cause momentary sadness but will not invoke the depth of feeling that the death of a sibling or close friend will bring. Members of the same family will experience the loss differently depending on their relationship with the deceased. One child may have been seen as the favored golden one and the other as the lost one. This will affect how they experience their parent's death. If an individual's sense of self-worth is tied up in the relationship, the grief may be more prolonged. This may happen in the loss of a spouse who provided security and a sense of well-being and purpose to the remaining spouse. They will struggle not just with the loss of the person, but the loss of a sense of self-esteem.

2. Personality Factors

Each person grieves differently, depending on their age, gender, coping style, ego strength, and world view. Children grieve differently from adults as their cognitive abilities and coping skills are less developed. While gender roles are less strictly observed than in previous generations, there is still the tendency for men to be expected to not show excessive emotion at the loss of a loved one. They are expected to be the strong ones who keep the family together while women are allowed to fall apart at the loss. Chances are we all know individuals who do not fit this stereotype in this age of gender fluidity; still there are enough that do to make this distinction relevant.

How a person copes is a stronger factor in how they grieve than gender. Some women as well as men don't allow themselves to show signs of grieving. Jackie Kennedy Onassis in the 1960s was a prime example of this as she bore the burden of publicly burying her husband, John F. Kennedy. She was upheld as a model of strength and grace under duress.

As a society we don't like messy displays of pain and so we are encouraged, like many of our British ancestors, to keep a stiff upper lip and reserve our emotions to times when away from prying eyes. Not everyone follows this norm. Some readily display emotions, others allow them to seep out slowly over time; still others repress feelings only to have them come out in unhealthy ways when they least expect it. Some people are more able to cope through problem solving; others may have a more optimistic outlook and find the positives in any given situation. While they actively grieve over a loss, they may acknowledge that they would not want their loved one back after a prolonged painful illness. They take comfort in knowing their loved one is no longer suffering.

Age is an important factor in how individuals experience grief. Young adults may have a fully formed understanding about death, but it is not on their radar unless forcibly brought to their attention through the loss of a loved one. They are focused on establishing themselves in careers and relationships, marrying and starting families. They are much too busy with life to think about death and all that entails. When it is forced on them, they may resist it.

I taught classes on Death and Dying for a period of ten years. The young adults in my class were usually there because it was required for their major. While there were some who were acquainted with death from past experience, most were uncomfortable with the topic and were reluctant to join in discussions. When the class visited a hospice home, one young adult hid in the back of the room next to the door, waiting to bolt as soon as the opportunity presented itself.

Middle-aged adults are becoming more aware that their time on this earth is limited. The loss of loved ones during this time brings that reality home to them. It might push them to reflect on their life and make changes, deciding what they want to do with the time they have left. (Children and Senior adults are covered in chapters 7 and 8, respectively.)

Individuals with a secure attachment style, who received adequate nurture and love as a child, will grieve differently from those with insecure attachment styles, who did not feel consistent, secure love from parents or guardians. Individuals with a strong sense of self and their own worth will recognize that while their pain is deep, it doesn't destroy who they are, their own value. They know that they can go on. Others without this sense of self-worth may feel like they don't exist without their loved one or don't know who they are; they question whether they can go on. As mentioned, this may be the case in marriages where one spouse received their self-worth through being part of a couple. After the loss of a spouse there is often a wondering about who you are without this significant person in your life, but in these individuals it is exacerbated.

Having a world view that supports the belief in life after death may help to ease the pain of a loss as survivors are reassured by the promise of seeing their loved one again. Certainly that has been my case with my Christian worldview. I was comforted in the loss of my friend and my dad by the thought that I would see them again someday. Deaths that threaten our world view may create a more complicated grieving and send the bereaved into a spiritual crisis. Someone who loses a child through an act of violence may question, where was God? This may lead them to no longer believe in God or to question whether God is good.

3. How the Person Died

The death of a loved one from natural causes after a long life is easier to accept than a sudden violent death of a young person. In the one case there would have been time to prepare and experience anticipatory grieving — grief experienced in anticipation of a loss. It also fit the expected norm for death. In the other, death came unexpectedly to someone who was not meant to die. This results in greater, more complicated grief. An act of violence can cause violent anger and grieving within the bereaved.

If the death was ambiguous without recovery of the body, such as in an air plane crash, the deceased's loved one may question, was my loved one actually on the plane? Without the evidence of a body, they may hold out hope that their loved one had not gotten on the plane. The difficulty in recovering bodies for victims of 9/11 made it harder for many of the bereaved to come to some sense of closure around the loss of their loved one. In situations of abductions or soldiers lost during the war, loved ones are put into the unbearable position of wondering for years whether their loved one is dead or alive, complicating their ability to grieve.

If the death was the result of violence, the legal system may become involved, further complicating the grieving process. The bereaved may have to deal with an investigation as police seek the offender, followed by the court case as they wait for a verdict. Some may feel unable to complete their grief until the one who murdered their loved one is tried and found guilty. If they have tried to move on, the long legal process may keep bringing back the pain. After the case is over, depending on the outcome they may feel some relief knowing the perpetrator of the crime has been punished, or they may be surprised when they don't obtain the relief they had thought they would receive with a conviction. If the suspect is acquitted or if no suspect is found, they may struggle to move beyond their anger.

If the death was stigmatized, such as a suicide or death from AIDS, the survivors are often deprived of social support after the death, since they aren't allowed to talk about it. While this has changed substantially over the years, there still remains some stigma attached to suicide and AIDS which complicates their loved one's bereavement.

4. History of Grief on part of Bereaved

Sometimes our grief is impacted by our past history of loss, especially if those losses were not adequately grieved at the time. Whenever we lose someone, it brings back to the surface other losses.

This is particularly the case with childhood losses because children are rarely able to completely understand and grieve losses from their childhood. While dealing with my divorce, issues from my childhood surfaced where they could be dealt with again, this time from a different perspective.

It can be helpful to understand how a person coped with losses in the past in order to understand why they are behaving the way they are in their current situation. My mom has her own way of coping with loss and grieving. It is not my way, but it is what works for her. Because I know historically how she deals with loss, I recognize what she is doing and allow her a certain amount of space to fall apart when she needs to, then I push her to get back up. Others may need help acknowledging what they have lost and allowing the pain to surface.

Sometimes when a person seems stuck in their grief after a loss, it may be because of unresolved grief from the past. It can be helpful to encourage them to remember those losses in order to work through them. This may be necessary before they can come to any sense of closure over their current loss.

5. Social Variables

Does the bereaved have a strong social network, perhaps through their church or work? Having such a network can help in the grieving process. It may not speed up the process, but it will help make the process easier. Having a pet has also been seen as a positive support to a person during grieving.

If the bereaved had a relationship with the deceased that was not socially recognized, such as a partner in a gay relationship that was not accepted by others, or the lover of a married person, they will not have the social support others receive. They experience disenfranchised grief — grief that is not acknowledged, that doesn't receive any social support. Cases of suicide and death from AIDS can result in disenfranchised grief, though this is less common today.

6. Concurrent Stressors

The final common factor influencing a person's grief is the other stressors that may come into play because of the loss. The loss of a spouse may result in the loss of home, financial struggles, and the need to find a job. Children who lose a parent may find themselves uprooted and sent to live with other family members, thereby exacerbating their loss through the loss of home, friends if moved into another school district, and the other parent if the remaining parent is too distressed to care for his/her children.

In the midst of trying to care for children and provide financially for their family, remaining spouses may find themselves overwhelmed by all of the losses. They may push aside their grief in order to take care of all the pressing demands of being a single parent, only to have the grief resurface later.

TASKS OR STAGES OF GRIEF

There are many different approaches to grief recovery, a number of stages or phases depending on which one you choose. Kubler-Ross's stages of dying are well known and apply to grief. There is the initial denial and shock when we hear a loved one has died, anger as we experience the hurt and loss and try to affix blame; bargaining as we try to find a way to alleviate our suffering or change the situation (this is especially prevalent in losses due to divorce, unemployment or ill health as we may bargain to change the outcome, not something one can do when a loved one has died); depression as we deal with all of the feelings related to our loss; and finally acceptance as we move on to a new life. Others talk of phases. Collin Murray Parkes notes four phases of mourning: a period of numbness, a time of yearning as the bereaved yearns for the lost one to return, a time of disorganization and despair, followed by a phase of reorganization. Others list five phases: shock, awareness of loss, conservation withdrawal, healing and renewal. Still others have their own lists.

All are useful, but I have found the approach taken by William Worden, in his book, *Grief Counseling and Grief Therapy*, as the most helpful.

Stages can imply that you move automatically through these states of grief; that "time" will heal all wounds. Time helps but it doesn't automatically heal. Some individuals live their life in a state of unresolved grief, unable to move on. The grief they experience remains as strong as on the day it first occurred. Any mention of their loved one brings back the grief as if it were yesterday. They are stuck.

Worden frames grief recovery in terms of four tasks to be completed. Tasks acknowledge that grief is work. It isn't enough to just let time slip by and hope to be healed. Healing from grief takes time and effort. There are tasks we need to do in order to progress through the loss. Tasks also empower individuals at a time when they feel helpless and vulnerable, awash in a sea of feelings that they don't understand and have difficulty controlling. Healing may not happen overnight, it will take time, but there are things you can do to help healing along. You are not just a helpless victim at the mercy of your feelings and memories.

The four tasks, according to Worden, are: 1. Accept the reality of the loss; 2. Process the pain; 3. Adjust to the world without the deceased; and 4. Find an enduring connection with the deceased while embarking on a new life. While acknowledging some of the stages of grief, I will be using Worden's four tasks to organize the passage through grief, assigning a chapter to each of the tasks. There is also a chapter on families and grief, children and grief, seniors and grief, and other losses as well as ways to help yourself and others as you pass through this difficult journey.

A number of faces of grief were described in this chapter. Before we move on to the next chapter, can you put a face on your grief? How are the six factors that affect grief influencing your grief? Write these down or share them with a friend or loved one.

Chapter 2

Accept the Reality

She was surprised when she opened the door.

"Is something wrong, officer?"

"Are you Sheryl Jones?"

"Yes, I am."

"Is your husband Brian Jones?"

"Yes, is he okay?"

"I'm afraid there has been an accident. Your husband didn't make it. We need you to identify the body."

"No, this can't be." Shock, disbelief, denial take over. "It can't be my Brian. Are you sure?"

"That's why we need you to come." Too upset to drive herself, she calls her son and together they go to the morgue.

"That's him," Jerry says as his mother sobs into his shoulder, clinging to him in disbelief.

And so begins the long, hard process of recovery from the loss of a loved one.

Despite seeing the body, Sheryl still feels that it is unreal. Her mind, not ready to accept the reality of his death and the full force of pain that goes with it, continues to insist it was a mistake, that she didn't see what she saw. Certainly it was just someone who looked like her Brian, even though the body had been pulled out of his car.

She goes through those first days in a state of shock. The visitation and the funeral are all a blur in her mind. She knows many people attended to offer her support at this difficult time, but their faces are just one sea of disembodied heads. She finds it hard to pull distinct faces from the mass. She reads the cards and looks at the signatures in the guest book so she guesses they were in attendance, she just doesn't remember. It still isn't real to her. She watches herself go through the motions of living as if it were someone else experiencing this loss, not her. She hears someone crying and wonders why, only to realize that someone is her.

"Why are you crying?" she asks herself. "It's only a bad dream. Soon you will wake up and Brian will be coming in the door for dinner the way he always does. You just have to wake up." She wakes and reaches over to Brian's side of the bed. Empty. So is her heart. There is a big empty void in her heart, a void only her husband can fill. Why doesn't he come home?

And so it goes, for days, weeks, as the inside struggle to grasp what has happened continues.

Denial, the first stage of Kubler-Ross's stages of dying, is a defense mechanism. It serves to protect the psyche from something that is just too painful to grasp all at once. It was too painful for Sheryl to accept that her husband was gone so she goes back and forth, in and out of denial, remaining in a protective cocoon of shock while her brain processes the information of her husband's death.

Around her are constant reminders of all she lost. The home she shared with her husband, the bed they slept in together, their children who rallied to her side to support her in her loss. Even though she saw the body at the morgue, that was through a haze of disbelief. She hadn't wanted to see the body during the visitation, yet she had to, custom dictated that. Still that wasn't her Brian. Her Brian had a smile that curled up around the side of his mouth, teasing her and daring her to smile back at him. That lifeless, cold body wasn't Brian. She would never assent to that, she told herself, yet seeing the body put her on the road to acceptance. It would take her weeks before she truly accepted the reality of her loss and all that would entail, but she was on the path to recovery from loss, the journey through grief.

The first task in this journey is accepting the reality of what you have lost. This isn't just the loss of the physical presence of your loved one, but the roles they filled in your life, all the parts that made up the whole relationship. We rarely know what a person means to us until they are gone. There are all of the little things we take for granted, the rituals you share: the way she clears her throat, the way he chortles, deep from his belly, rather than letting loose with a loud guffaw, the way he saves the last bite of dessert for her, the way she knows how to get him out of a funk and laughing. All of these make up a relationship. All of this is gone with the death of one of the members.

Sheryl hadn't just lost a husband, she lost her best friend, her companion, the one she had shared so much of her life with, the one she expected to share the remainder of her life with, growing old together, the father of her children. She had lost her past, the memories she shared only with him, and she had lost her future, the one they had planned together. She had lost her dreams, as well as all the other roles Brian played in her life: lover, decision-maker, provider, the list goes on as she slowly comes to face reality.

Seeing the body and the funeral are important first steps in the journey to acceptance. They are concrete expressions of what was lost. In situations where there is no body, such as victims of a plane crash where no bodies are recovered, or a fiery car crash where the body is burned beyond recognition, it can be harder to reach acceptance that their loved one is gone. They may know intellectually, but there remains a part of them that may refuse to believe. They get stuck in this stage of the grieving process and find it hard to move on.

As more people choose cremation for their loved ones and forego a viewing, the question arises how this might impact the grief process for those left behind. In the case of a sudden, unexpected death such as Brian's, seeing the body is crucial. In a situation of a long illness where family have adequate time to prepare for death, it may not be as important as family may have gathered around their loved one as death approached to say goodbye, or even been present at the moment of death and seen the body being taken away. Even in cases of cremation, some families choose to have a viewing, allowing those who come to have a chance for a final farewell and the ability to confront the reality that their loved one has died.

The funeral is also an important ritual to begin the healing process. It is a rite of transition. The community gathers around the family of the deceased in order to offer support. VanGenep speaks of rites of passages as situations where a person goes from one state to another state. For example, in marriage, two single individuals go through a ritual, the wedding ceremony, and come out on the other side, no longer single, but part of a couple. There is a celebratory meal to mark the occasion.

With funerals, you have an intact family that has just lost a member of that family. They go through a ritual, the funeral service where their loved one's life is remembered and celebrated, tears flow, then the body is taken on a final journey to the cemetery where it is left. The family returns from the cemetery without their loved one, symbolically leaving the loved one behind, returning as a new family. They gather with the community afterwards and share a meal. The process facilitates the change in the family from one with the deceased member to one without that member. In the case of Brian's situation, the transition was from a family with a married couple, to a single adult household. The family is re-incorporated into the community through the ritual and the sharing of a meal.

The funeral plays an important role in the grief process not only by helping families accept the reality, but it gives an opportunity to express feelings of sadness (task 2), assign meaning to the loss through the words of the minister (task 3) and begins the work of adjusting to the world without their loved one (task 3).

In order to complete the task of accepting the reality of the loss, the bereaved needs time to recognize what she/he has lost. It will be different for each person depending on who the deceased was to them. For Sheryl, the deceased was her husband. For her grown children, he was their father. Even though they are grown and on their own, this is a significant loss. Perhaps he was the one they called on for advice when faced with career choices or financial decisions. This advice is no longer available to them. Perhaps he helped with home improvement projects at their homes. Perhaps he had become a friend, not just a father. With his death a part of them is gone.

Brian's mother has lost her son. No matter how old our children are, they are always our children.

This loss is the source of great pain. It upsets the natural course of life. Parents aren't supposed to outlive their children. It robs them of part of their legacy to the world and of a source of support in old age. Perhaps they relied on their child to take care of financial matters and help around the house. Perhaps their child was a source of comfort, visiting them on days off, or stopping by to chat after work. All of this is gone with their child's death.

Brian's siblings have lost a brother, someone who knows what it was to grow up in their home. Someone who shared memories only they had, memories they don't have with their spouses. Perhaps he was a support in caring for their aging parents. Now that support is gone. And Brian's grandchildren have lost a grandfather, a source of unconditional love. Perhaps he was the one who took them fishing or who showed up at all of the sporting events or school activities to cheer them on.

All of the people in Brian's life have to come to terms with what they lost as part of accepting this reality and moving through the journey.

How to Help

How can you help someone with this first task? First by showing up at the visitation and funeral, being available to talk if needed, or to sit in silence with them if that is what they need. When talking to them, don't use euphemisms that hide the reality, like he has passed away or has gone. Use the D word – dead.

We live in a society that denies death, covering up with euphemisms, embalming and painting the face of the deceased lest they look dead. And if that is too much, we can cremate the body so no one need be bothered by this uncomfortable reality. We need to help people in denial, living in a society in denial, to break through that denial when they are ready.

It is after the funeral, when all of the loved ones have dispersed to their own homes and their own lives, that this reality comes crashing down around the person. This is an essential part of the mourning process, but that doesn't make it easy. It can be helpful to check in on the person in the weeks after a death to see how they are coping. Ask them about the events around the death. You may think you already know this, or that it may be too painful for them to talk about those events, but reliving them with someone who cares and listens is one way to help them process the events and make sense of them. Encourage them to talk about all they have lost. Share memories of their loved one with them. Ask them about how they met, the early years of their relationship. Talking about their loved one is a way to help the bereaved accept the reality that their loved one is gone and move onto the next task — processing the pain.

Chapter 3

Process the Pain

It has been a month since Brian's death and Sheryl can't seem to stop crying. Everywhere she looks are reminders of Brian and all that she lost: his toothbrush, his shaving cream and aftershave, his clothes. Sometimes she goes into his closet and breathes in the smell of his clothes. She thinks, how can he be gone when I can still smell his presence? She longs to return to the numbness she had felt during the funeral. It was easier then. Her sleep is disrupted as she wakes up in the middle of the night and is unable to return to sleep because her brain is flooded with memories.

"Maybe I should ask the doctor for something. Some pain meds, or sleeping pills," she says to her daughter when she calls to check on her mom.

"I'll be over this weekend, Mom. We can talk about it then."

As denial gives way to acceptance, the feelings that had been held back by the denial come to the surface. Some people may resist those feelings by denying the significance of the death. Perhaps Brian had a troubled relationship with his daughter, to the point that she had cut him out of her life. She may come dutifully to the funeral to support her mother, but refuse to acknowledge any loss.

"We didn't get along," she may tell her husband when he asks how she is doing. "I lost him years ago when I cut him out of my life. I grieved then. I'm not grieving now." She may be hiding from her feelings, feelings of guilt about the relationship and how she had cut him out of her life and her children's life. Guilt that now she will never be able to have the relationship with her dad that she had once hoped for.

It's not healthy to deny feelings. They have a way of coming out in unhealthy ways, through physical symptoms and health problems. Anger we are holding in may come out as an ulcer or a clenched jaw that creates pain. Some may seek to medicate the pain away with alcohol or drugs, but all that does is prolong the healing process as once the medication is gone, the feelings come back to the surface, long after the support network may be gone.

Let's say Sheryl talks her physician into giving her something to dull the pain. She may go for months before her doctor discontinues the drugs. By then her family and friends have moved on significantly from their grief and figure Sheryl has too. All the feelings come rushing back, but now, Sheryl has less support. Her support network is no longer available as they were during the first months of her loss. Better to feel the pain as it surfaces rather than to medicate it away.

Following are some of the common feelings experienced by people as they grieve.

Sadness

That the bereaved will feel sad is understood. This may be expressed in tears, but not always. There may be violent bouts of sobs or a quiet trace of tears. Sometimes the bereaved may be afraid of the intensity of the sadness and hold back from expressing this. They fear that others will be uncomfortable with their feelings and so hold them back until they are able to let them out alone, crying into pillows at night. At the same time they may long to be able to cry with others and receive the moral support that tears often elicit.

One of the benefits of the funeral is that it provides a space where it is okay to shed tears. Unfortunately in our society, the normal amount of time given for bereavement leave is three days. This is hardly sufficient to grieve a loved one. The shock of the loss is often just beginning to abate after three days. Even in cases where the death is expected, there is a sense of shock when it finally happens. When a person expresses sadness for months after a loss, those around them may not be as receptive, thinking she should be over it by then. This is when a grief support group may be helpful, providing a safe place to talk about the loss and share tears when appropriate, share and celebrate small steps toward recovery. During the early weeks after a loss, the feelings are usually too fresh to benefit from a group setting. After around three months, individuals are more likely to benefit, though it varies based on the situation and the person.

Anger

Sheryl stares at the pile of bills on her table as she attempts to balance the checkbook. She throws the checkbook across the room.

"Damn you, Brian Jones!"

"Mom, what are you doing?" Her daughter comes out of the other room where she is going through her dad's belongings.

"How could your dad leave me like this? He knows I'm no good at numbers. He always took care of the bills. I'm so angry at him. I'll never forgive him for leaving me."

Anger is the second stage of Kubler-Ross's stages of dying. You might ask, how can Sheryl be angry at Brian for dying? It wasn't his choice. But feelings aren't logical. There is a close connection between hurt and anger. When we are hurting, we feel anger and want to lash out, blame someone, anyone. It's common for people in grief to get angry at the loved one for leaving them. And if their loved one had any part in their own death, the alcoholic who continues to drink and drive despite repeated warnings, who dies in a car accident, or if Brian was checking a text when his car went off the road, or the worst case scenario, a suicide where the deceased takes his own life, the anger increases exponentially.

If the bereaved doesn't get angry at their loved one, they may get angry at the doctor, especially if there was any indication of malpractice. They may start a crusade against the drunk driver that took their loved one's life, or anyone who might be held in any part responsible for the death. They may be angry at God for taking their loved one. Or they may turn the anger against themselves, sinking into depression or considering hurting themselves.

They need to find healthy ways to let their anger out, whether shouting in their empty home or pounding on a pillow, anything that works but doesn't harm themselves or others. The anger may give way to sobs as pain arises once again. All are a normal part of the grieving process.

Guilt

"Brian was going to the store for me," Sheryl cried. "If I hadn't sent him to the store, he would still be alive." Sheryl tortured herself with the memory.

Guilt, real or imagined, is common after a loss. The bereaved may feel guilty for things done or not done. They may feel guilty that they had not been kind enough to their loved one, had neglected them or had fought with them. Adult children that live far away from their parents may feel guilt for not being around at the time of death or for not visiting enough. Spouses may feel they didn't do enough and feel guilt over not being present when a loved one dies.

One son, whose father died alone unexpectedly at night in the hospital, was determined not to let this happen with his mother. Out of feelings of guilt over his father's death, he refused to leave her side when she was hospitalized, to the detriment of his health and well-being. Others have stayed by a loved one's side through the dying process, determined to be there at the end, only to have their loved one slip away when they leave for a short time to get something to eat or when they fall asleep.

They can torment themselves with guilt over not being there at the end, not recognizing that their loved one may not have felt free to leave as long as they were there. To them, you might say, "For some people, they find it too difficult to leave if their loved ones are present, so they wait until they are gone to slip away." This helps explain the situation and provide comfort.

Guilt that is imagined can be reality tested.

"I just didn't do enough," they may say.

"What did you do?" After they relate the list of what they did, you can point out, "Sounds like you did a lot."

If they feel guilty about unkind words said before a death, point out how this was one incident, that the deceased knows how much they loved them.

In Sheryl's case, you might explore how much Brian liked to help out. Invite her to tell you more about what happened that morning, more about Brian.

"That's just the way Brian was. He was always running errands. He liked going to the store. Sometimes it took him two hours to get a loaf of bread. He would run into someone he knew and talk for an hour or more before coming home."

"So you didn't exactly force Brian to go to the store for you?"

"No, I guess not. If he hadn't been going to the store to pick up something for me, he probably would have found some other excuse to go there."

Adult children who feel guilty over not being around more may be encouraged to recognize what they did do, how they called every week or came for a week at a time when they did visit. Others may need help forgiving themselves, despite reassurance that their loved one understood.

"Your dad was always so proud of you and your independence," Sheryl told her youngest daughter who lived across the country from them.

"Even though I lived so far from home?"

"He missed you, we both missed you, but we were proud of you for what you were doing with your life."

Situations where guilt is warranted may lead to a situation of complicated grief, requiring professional help.

Survivor guilt – sometimes people feel guilty for surviving when their loved one didn't. This can happen in situations of car crashes or any accident that takes some lives and leaves others. Survivors of war often experience guilt for coming home when their buddies didn't make it. Parents feel guilty for living when their children have died. If it had been in their power, they would have given their life for their child, but it wasn't in their power to do this. Still they feel guilt.

Fear and Anxiety

"I never knew grief was so much like fear," C.S. Lewis tells us in his book, *A Grief Observed*, about the loss of his wife. Fear is a common feeling associated with grief.

As Sheryl confronted the many tasks she now had to take on, she wondered, could she do it? Was life worth living without Brian in it? She also worried — life was so fragile. It can end at any moment. Her children felt it too, worrying about having another loved one snatched away by death through an accident. The death of someone we love brings home the reality that we, too, will someday die. It is difficult to look death in the face. This may bring to the surface fears we weren't aware of. We often go about this life unaware of what is truly going on around us as we are caught up in the events of daily life, our jobs, caring for our home, our loved one.

Death forces us to look, even if for but a moment, at the bigger picture, the bigger questions. This can be a blessing, but it also can bring fears to the surface as we confront our mortality.

Anxiety is free-floating fear, fear not attached to a cause. In the case of the death of a loved one, the anxiety may be over whether they will be okay and their own heightened awareness of death. The bereaved may feel anxiety but not be aware of where it is coming from. They may need help attaching the anxiety to a fear and reality testing that fear. Yes, death does come to all of us, but that doesn't mean we can't live a fulfilled, meaningful life for as long as we have. That doesn't mean we have to let fear keep us from living our life.

Loneliness

Even though Sheryl had a wide network of friends from work and church, providing a buffer against social loneliness, they couldn't counteract the emotional loneliness she felt after Brian's loss. She yearned for his embrace, to feel his gentle touch on her shoulder as he passed by her in the kitchen, his kiss as he left for work. Being out with her friends, seeing couples together, sometimes left her feeling even more alone as it brought to the forefront what she had lost. And so she would stay home rather than accept friends' invitations to go to dinner or see a movie.

In some cases, widows and widowers find themselves without their circle of friends as they become the third person in what used to be two couples, or the fifth person in a circle of three couples, upsetting the balance of the group. Married couples may see the surviving spouse as a reminder of what could happen to them, or, especially in situations of divorce, may see the now single adult as a potential threat to their marriage. And so the person experiencing emotional loneliness from the loss of their loved one may find themselves bereft of their circle of friends and thrust into social loneliness as well.

Helplessness

Sometimes, in the midst of great loss, we can feel helpless, unable to do activities we once did with ease, unable to keep going. We are all helpless when confronted with the ultimate reality of death. We feel helpless to change the situation, to bring our loved one back to us, which then translates into feeling helpless in other areas of life. We can confront those feelings by encouraging the bereaved to recognize their ability, challenging them to do what they can do. Trying to relieve a loved one of all responsibility because of feelings of helplessness only feeds those feelings, letting them know they truly are unable to do for themselves. It can be a balancing act for loved ones to know when to assist the bereaved and when to insist that they do something themselves.

Relief

In situations where a loved one has been sick for a long time, their loved ones may feel relief that their suffering is over. They may also feel relief that they no longer have to care for their loved one, and then feel guilty over this natural feeling. If the relationship was strained, they may be relieved to know this difficult person is no longer in their life, having to be contended with, and again feeling guilt over this feeling.

How to Help

Helping someone process these feelings requires a balance of sympathetic listening, supporting the bereaved as they experience their feelings, acknowledging the depth of their loss, and then bringing them out of the feelings into practical considerations. Feelings need to be accepted, but the individual must not be left drowning in a sea of feelings.

If the individual is not allowing their feelings to surface, they might be encouraged to appear, but only if you are comfortable dealing with the strong feelings that may surface and have sufficient time to stay with the person and their feelings. Sometimes a kind word or an expression of sympathy is all it takes to get tears flowing. Once the tears are present, stay with the person until the tears are no longer flowing freely. To encourage someone to grieve then leave them unsupported in that state is not helpful.

Often the bereaved one is fearful of the strength of their own feelings and have worked hard to control them for good reason. Once they let loose they may fear they will not be able to get them under control again. This is where the concept of "dosing" is helpful. The idea is to allow feelings to surface one dose at a time, as the individual feels able to deal with the feelings. Another way to manage feelings is to balance between allowing the feelings to come to the surface, then pushing them back through focusing on practical aspects of life. This gets the bereaved out of the feelings and into their mind in order to go on with life.

Whatever feeling they may be experiencing, acknowledge the feeling and help them recognize it is a normal part of the grieving process. If they feel relief and then feel guilty over this feeling, let them know it is normal to feel relief at times. It doesn't mean they didn't love the deceased. If they are feeling helpless, again let them know this is normal and show them the many ways in which they have been coping and showing themselves far from helpless. Support them in their loneliness, assuring them that this is a normal part of loss and will diminish over time.

If the bereaved is unaware of anger they may be harboring, or they are suppressing these feelings, you can help them get in touch with this anger by asking, "What don't you miss about your loved one?"

"What do you mean? I miss everything about him/her?" they may respond.

"There must be something you don't miss."

"Well, I guess I don't miss picking up after him. He always left his dirty underwear on the floor." Or "I don't miss her trying to tell me what to do." One item will lead to another.

Often after a death, the deceased is wrapped in an aura of "goodness." It is considered wrong to speak ill of the dead so family members insist on remembering only the good times and positive traits of their loved one. But this leaves the deceased a one-dimensional figment of imagination, not the whole, two-dimensional being they were in life. To only remember the good is not helpful to the grieving process. The bereaved needs to remember their loved one as they truly were. How can one be angry at a saint, someone who was perfect in every way?

If the bereaved had a conflicted relationship with the deceased, they may struggle to remember anything good about the person. This can be equally detrimental to the grieving process. It can be a way to hide from their pain by insisting they are not affected by the loss. In this case it can be helpful to ask, "What do you miss?"

They may insist they don't miss anything but if you persist they will likely be able to come up with something. In the case of a child estranged from their parent, what they may miss is the possibility of the relationship being different. That can be the starting point for them to recognize their loss and start the grieving process.

Depression

One final note on depression before we leave the broad category of feelings. Depression is the fourth stage of the Kubler-Ross stages of dying. Depression is more than sadness. You can feel sad, but not be depressed. When my mom lost her second husband, she complained of crying all the time, yet scored as not being depressed when tested, as opposed to a year earlier when she had been dealing with my stepfather's failing health. My mom was sad, yes, but not depressed. The burden of caregiving had been lifted off of her and even though she missed him, she started doing activities she had not been able to do while he was alive and actively engaging in her life again.

Symptoms of depression parallel those found in grief: loss of appetite, sleep disturbance, intense sadness, difficulty concentrating and inability to make decisions; however, in grief there is not the loss of self-esteem that is found in clinical depression. Grief can lead to depression, but in and of itself it is not depression. This is an important distinction to make. The depression of Kubler-Ross's stages is a morass of feelings that can overwhelm the individual. Depression can come from anger turned inward or from unresolved, complicated grief that hangs on for longer than what would be considered normal. Worden states, "Freud believed that in grief, the world looks poor and empty, while in depression, the person feels poor and empty," (p. 32) helpful distinctions.

One of the signs that grieving has progressed to clinical depression is that normal feelings associated with grieving are exaggerated from what would be normally expected — i.e., guilt goes beyond guilt over actions taken or not taken at time of the death to feeling guilty about every aspect of their life; anxiety and thoughts of death go beyond what normally occurs; there is morbid preoccupation with their worthlessness indicating loss of self-esteem and hallucinations beyond seeing their deceased loved one or hearing their voice. Most individuals are able to move through the sadness associated with loss without becoming clinically depressed. If clinical depression is suspected, then professional help is recommended.

Grieving is hard work. The feelings are many, conflicting and confusing. We have dealt with the most common ones. Sometimes the bereaved needs time to dwell on their losses and experience their feelings, whatever those feelings may be. Other times they need diversions to get their mind off of their loss. It's a balancing act that family members can help with if they are attuned to the grieving process and what their loved one may need at any given moment. This means sometimes listening to their feelings, other times getting them out of the house for a needed diversion, and other times helping them deal with the practical realities of adjusting to life without their loved ones.

Chapter 4

Adjust to Life without your Loved One

"There's so much to do," Sheryl tells her daughter as she struggles to put her life back into some semblance of normalcy. Besides taking on the finances, there are all the responsibilities she had left to Brian to handle over the years. He was the one with a knack for mechanical repairs. Not only did she have to mow the lawn, now she had to learn how to replace spark plugs when the lawn mower stopped firing, or call on her son or hire someone to do it for her.

She had been reluctant to even try at first, she had felt so lost, and the mere thought of everything overwhelmed her so that she wanted to climb back into bed and stay there. But after she got over her initial resistance to attempting to do the small repairs around the house, she was finding she could be handy and found a new sense of self-worth and accomplishment. Even as she felt accomplishment, she was beset by guilt by being able to feel good about doing something Brian once did.

The checkbook had seemed like just a jumble of random numbers. She was always bouncing checks until, with the help of her son, she was able to come up with a system that worked for her. Brian had been a good provider and continued to be so after his death. He had multiple accounts and retirement income stashed away. She wouldn't have to worry about money, didn't even need to continue to work if she didn't want to. She was better off than so many of her single friends.

There are many adjustments that need to be made to accommodate to a life without a loved one. There are all of the external roles and responsibilities they filled, and there are the more subtle, yet very important, internal adjustments that need to be made.

As Sheryl adjusted to her life as a widow, she had to either take on roles filled by her husband or find someone else to do them. This means doing the cooking if he was the chef in the family, mowing the lawn, running errands, taking care of the finances, whatever else your spouse used to do. It also means you take on the role of the bereaved, becoming a widow or widower. The bereaved may be pushed into an identity crisis much like the one experienced during the teen years.

"I've been part of a couple for over thirty years. I don't know how to be a single," the survivor may say. The new role will feel awkward, uncomfortable. It won't fit at first as they struggle to know who they are without their loved one.

While Sheryl is fortunate to not have to work, many others find themselves plunged into poverty at the death of a spouse and need to either find employment, or take on additional work in order to pay household bills. If the deceased left young children at home, the remaining spouse may struggle with accepting the identity of a single parent and the need to fill parenting roles filled by their spouse. Perhaps a grandparent or aunt or uncle may be available to help out and provide a role model of the same gender as the deceased for the children.

Who takes the children to school and picks them up will need to be worked out. Who makes school lunches, who stays home with sick children. Perhaps an older child may take on some of the responsibility for caring for younger siblings. The responsibility of caring for young children may seem like an overwhelming burden, or it could be a life saver. At the time of loss, the remaining spouse may want to sink into a vat of despair, stop functioning, stop going to work, but the presence of children who need care can force them to keep going, give them a reason for being when it feels like their life has lost all purpose.

Often the pain is so great that individuals want to make drastic changes in an attempt to run away from the pain. They may throw out every item of clothing, every belonging that reminds them of the deceased, sell the house and move away. However, what is a painful reminder at first may be a source of comfort later, when the freshness of the loss abates. They may look for a piece of clothing or an object to hold onto as a remembrance or regret a move that cannot be undone. If they move to a new community, they will be forced to go through the grief process without the benefit of their social circle of friends.

It is not recommended that the bereaved make any major changes during the first year after a major loss. Grieving is a bit like going crazy. After a while they will come to their old selves and may regret decisions made when they were not in their right mind.

During task three, the bereaved may struggle to find meaning in the loss. This can be especially difficult if the deceased was the victim of an act of violence or met an untimely death. The bereaved struggles to understand why this happened. Their world view may be turned upside down. The world that was once a safe and secure place, is no longer so. As mentioned, the funeral can help with this process of finding meaning. A well-thought-out and sincere eulogy or sermon that sums up the person's life in an honest, loving way can begin this process. By the same token, a thoughtless, generic sermon or the lack of a eulogy will be remembered and not favorably. As a former pastor, I've been told and have told others, church members will forgive you a multitude of sins as long as you care for them and their family at the time of loss. The reverse is also true. I know people who were so offended by a perceived slight at the time of a loved one's death, that they left that church entirely, or stayed but never forgave that particular minister their failings.

Sometimes adjusting to life without a loved one requires an adjustment in worldview. Someone who was not spiritual at the time of loss may find comfort and support in religious beliefs, while another may seek to understand a world where young people are taken prematurely or a world of violence and be thrown into a crisis of faith. Some may struggle with unfinished business and need help with this. Others may struggle to find forgiveness, perhaps of themselves or their loved one, before they can move on.

Dealing with Holidays and Anniversaries

"I wish I could just skip Christmas this year," my eighty-five year old mother tells me. She had lost her second husband the past September and while they had been married less than five years, the pain remained. A friend of mine's dad died just before Thanksgiving this year, leaving her lost without the man in her life who holds a place no one else can hold and no one can fill. Each grieve over the empty place at the dinner table over the holidays.

As mentioned, grief is hard work. It takes time and energy. This work is made harder by the holidays and memories of past holidays and all you have lost. The pressure to be "merry" may leave you feeling like crawling into a hole and only coming out after the holidays are over. People experiencing grief often want to get through the pain as quickly as possible, but try though we might, we can't make the days go by any faster and we can't just jump over the month of December to skip the holiday.

What we can do is not let the holidays and the pressure to celebrate run our life or ruin each day. As C.S. Lewis said, "The pain now is part of the happiness before. That's the deal." If you are feeling sorrow, it is precisely because you loved the deceased. It's all part of the package. You can't have one without the other.

Unwrap the gift of grief slowly, intentionally, or rip it open quickly. Whatever works for you. Remind yourself and your loved one that the grief you feel is a gift; it is proof that you have loved and loved deeply. Keep traditions that you want to preserve, but don't be afraid to let go of other traditions and create new ones. If having a Christmas tree is a painful reminder of all of the trees you decorated together, then forego a tree. If you don't feel up to going to parties, then stay home or opt for a small gathering of friends and/or family. Sometimes grieving requires time alone to allow feelings to surface; other times, being with friends and family is a needed break from the work of grieving. Be open to both.

Birthdays and anniversaries will also be a challenge during the first year after a loss. Wedding anniversaries for widows and widowers can be especially painful. The bereaved may want to schedule a diversion to help them get through those days, or they may simply want to spend the time alone at home, remembering their loved one and grieving what they have lost. These days can be both painful reminders of your loss, and a welcome opportunity to remember your loved one, especially as the years pass. Each year I welcome my dad's birthday as an opportunity to remember him.

While loss of a loved one is acutely felt over the holidays and on other special days, these days will pass. Each year it will become easier. Be kind to yourself during these times.

How to Help

Family can help the bereaved by assuming some of the tasks filled by the deceased or helping the bereaved with their chores until they are able to do them themselves. They can help the bereaved make plans, figure out what needs to be done, and who can do this. They can listen as the bereaved struggles to make sense of their world without their loved one and all that entails. The tradition of bringing over a meal to relieve the bereaved of that chore continues to be a helpful way to express support for a loved one. Offering to watch children if young children are involved can also be a source of help.

A kind note or a call over the holidays or when an anniversary approaches is a welcome reminder that they are not alone, that their loss has not been forgotten. It can be helpful to mark these significant dates on a calendar. It is especially important to note the anniversary of the loss and offer support to the bereaved at that time. As life around them goes on and it seems everyone has forgotten about their loss, taking time to acknowledge this loss and giving them the opportunity to talk about their loved one, if they want, can be helpful.

All four of the tasks of mourning may go on at the same time. It is not a matter of moving from one task to the next. This is especially true of tasks two and three. They will need to be handled concurrently. While in the midst of dealing with intense sadness, there are still chores to be done. Children need to be cared for, bills need to be paid, laundry done. Doing these chores can help keep a person from sinking into a state of depression and inactivity that would be detrimental to them and those around them. It is helpful to alternate between the two tasks as the bereaved journeys through grief to new life, new beginnings.

Chapter 5

Find an Enduring Connection with the Deceased

Nothing can make up for the absence of someone whom we love, and it would be wrong to try to find a substitute; we must simply hold out and see it through. That sounds very hard at first, but at the same time it is a great consolation, for the gap, if it remains unfilled, preserves the bond between us. It is nonsense to say that God fills the gap. He doesn't fill it, but on the contrary, He keeps it empty and so helps us keep alive our former communion with each other, even at the cost of pain. – Dietrich Bonhoeffer

It has been over a year since Brian's death. Sheryl can't believe it has already been a year. Some days it feels like it was just yesterday when she had heard that fateful knock on the door. Other days it feels like an eternity.

"How long does it take?" she asks her pastor.

"It takes as long as it takes," she responds.

Often the deceased want a time line. They want to know when they will start feeling better. There is no set timeline. How long it takes depends on many factors, all those mentioned in chapter one and more. All contribute to the individual time line for healing.

Sheryl made it through all of those firsts. The first Christmas alone, the first Thanksgiving, the first anniversary, other important dates throughout the year. After the anniversary of his death, she thought it would get better, only to be thrown into a panic when she realized she had gone for almost a whole day without thinking about her husband.

"What if I forget him?" she asks. She's afraid of losing so many precious memories.

There was a time when counselors encouraged the bereaved to let go of their loved one in order to form new relationships. What they have discovered is that this is not how grief works. The bereaved continue to hold onto their loved ones. To insist that they let go was not helpful. What was helpful was assisting the bereaved in finding a way to hold onto their loved one while embarking on a new life.

I still remember my dad, especially any time the Michigan State Spartans are playing football or basketball. My dad loved to watch the Spartans. He was buried in a Spartan sweatshirt. So now I reconnect with my dad by watching the team he loved. I also have an oversized Spartan jacket of my dad's that I wear on occasion. When I wear it, it's as if I'm being wrapped in his arms. Others find their own way of reconnecting with their deceased loved one. This doesn't keep us from moving on and embracing new relationships.

Sheryl has cleared out most of Brian's clothes. The clothes her son and sons-in-law did not want were given to Goodwill. But she keeps a couple of his sweaters to wear during the cold of winter. Pictures still maintain a prominent place in her home, but she is no longer keeping a shrine to her husband. She has kept active in her church and in her grandchildren's activities and recently began a part-time job at a local non-profit, not because she needed the money, but because she wanted something else to do with her time. She has even considered dating some of the single men from her church. At first she felt unfaithful even considering this, but she has finally allowed herself to do this. No one can replace Brian. No one has the history with her that Brian has. But perhaps there is someone else that she can spend time with. Perhaps there is someone else she can love in a different way than she loved Brian. Brian would have wanted her to go on with her life, just as she would have wanted him to find someone else to love if she had been the one to die first.

She doesn't know that she will marry again, but after two years, she has fashioned a life for herself without her husband and it is a good life. She still misses him, wishes he were still here, but since he is not coming back, she has made the choice to go on with her life, whatever that may mean, and to live what she has left to the fullest. She has come through denial, anger, bargaining, and depression to acceptance.

What does embracing a new life look like? Some may think it is finding another person to love. Others may think that if a newly bereaved person remarries too soon, it indicates they didn't love their spouse. While it is not advisable to rush into a new relationship, waiting until all four tasks are completed isn't always necessary before entering a new relationship. In cases of a prolonged illness, the remaining spouse may have had time to grieve the dying spouse over the course of the illness and so may be further along in the grieving process than someone who loses a spouse unexpectedly. Sometimes the new relationship can be a source of support as they complete the tasks.

Some have said that women grieve, while men get a replacement spouse. Statistically men do have a tendency to remarry sooner than women but this doesn't necessarily indicate a lack of love or inadequate grieving. If the marriage was a good one, they may miss what they had and seek to find that again with another individual. It can be a tribute to the happiness they experienced with their first wife that they want to find that again. I had a friend whose wife died before Thanksgiving. By the next Easter, he remarried a wonderful woman well suited to him. His wife had been ill for years before her death. He took care of her. There was no unfinished business between them. He loved being married and so he sought to have that closeness again with someone else, with her blessing if she had been around to give it.

Individuals don't go through these tasks in a sequential fashion. They may go back and forth or work on all four at the same time. How do you know when you are done grieving? When you have come to acceptance that your beloved is no longer in your life, have found a way to keep them in your heart, and have moved on. There is no set timeline for this or one way to determine you have finished, and nothing says you can't go back after you thought you were finished. Only you determine when you are done.

Complicated Grief

Most are able to make it through grief with minimal outside support. Some say to suggest anyone who is grieving needs to see a counselor is to medicalize normal grief, making it a condition or ailment that needs to be cured rather than a normal human process. Sometimes, though, the bereaved may feel stuck, unable to move through grief and thus in need of more formal support.

How do you know whether you are dealing with normal grief or complicated grief? If the person is stuck in any one of the four tasks, that may indicate complicated grief. Perhaps it's been six months but they still can't believe their loved one is gone. Or they are stuck in the pain. Their grief is as strong one year later as during the first months. They don't seem to be moving forward. They have not adjusted to the loss or taken on any of the roles left empty by their loved one.

Sometimes it appears that the grief is greater than what might be expected for the situation, as when a co-worker dies and one grieves as if it had been a close friend. It might be that the loss has brought up unresolved losses from their past. If the bereaved had a conflicted relationship with the person, they may struggle to resolve those conflicts now that the person is gone. If it has been years and they have not moved on, but continue to grieve as if it had been yesterday, they may need professional help to remove the blocks that are keeping them from completing their grief.

Some may need help forgiving their loved one for things done or not done in the past. Others may need help forgiving themselves for actions on their part. A member of the clergy or a trained counselor can help them explore these issues and find the forgiveness they need.

How to help

Supportive words as the bereaved makes tentative steps forward are helpful. Assure them that it is okay to move one, that it doesn't mean they didn't love the deceased. Support them in their search to find a place for their deceased loved one. It can be by supporting a cause they believed in or by establishing a ritual of remembrance on significant days. Anything that helps them remember their loved one in a way that allows them to move forward. Grieve with them in their loss, rejoice with them in their new life.

Chapter 6

Families and Grief

Families are great. They are the building block of society, the primary means of support and connection for the vast majority of people. But families are also messy.

One of the first places we may look for support after a loss is our family. The problem is that if the deceased is a family member, each member is also grieving. All the more reason to look to them for support, you may think, however it doesn't always work that way. Each person's relationship with the deceased is uniquely their own, not the same as any other. And everyone grieves differently. Where one person may feel the need to talk, cry and express their feelings, another may need to find healing through silence, withdrawing inside their self. Clearly this sets up a situation of conflict.

While family members may bond together over tears and memories at the time of the funeral, each will have to take their own journey through grief, a journey that may not coincide with the journey of other family members. Sharing a home with someone who is actively grieving can be a challenge. Complicate this by several people who are grieving and you have treacherous waters. That's why family members need help outside of the family, whether from friends, clergy or counselors.

Sheryl found that her need to express the depths of her grief over Brian's death upset her children at times. She didn't feel she needed a counselor, but she did decide to go to a grief support group at her church. There she found others who were grieving and a safe place to share her feelings. The handouts and information provided by the group leader helped her realize she wasn't going crazy, helped to normalize her grief. The group provided a social network that supported her in her grieving process. There she could talk about things she couldn't talk about with family and friends. She could tell her children were wondering when she would get over this, when she would get back to normal. She wondered this too. With the members of the support group she didn't have to pretend to be okay when she wasn't.

Friends and family may be uncomfortable around them, not knowing whether to say something or not. The bereaved may long to talk about their loved one and appreciate the invitation at one time, and not want to talk other times. This can leave friends and family feeling caught in a no-win situation. Their loved one may feel hurt and angry if they don't bring up the deceased's name and hurt and angry when they do.

Our society isn't geared to support grief. There are no social structures to help the bereaved navigate these waters. The time when the bereaved wore black for a year after a death is over. This doesn't mean they don't need that time. They may walk the streets of their hometown, go to the local grocery store, and feel out of place. It may feel unfamiliar. They may want to grab the people around them and shake them and let them know that life is not the same as it was before their loved one died. How can they go about life as if nothing had happened, they may question. Some suggest that we need a sign that a person has experienced a loss, perhaps a black armband. This would alert those around them to the fact that they are grieving. When they are ready, the bereaved can remove the arm band as a sign that they are no longer actively grieving.

Loss of a Spouse

Each member of a family fills multiple roles. Brian was a husband to Sheryl, father to their three children, grandfather, brother, uncle and a beloved son to his mother. Each member of his family will grieve his loss in their own way.

We've already seen the impact on Sheryl as his wife. She lost her best friend, lover, co-parent, financial provider, her present that she shared with him, the future they had planned together. The hopes and dreams that they had shared are now shattered and she is left to pick up the pieces. While she still has her memories of their life together, no one else shared all of these memories. She may have lost her circle of friends as the couples they socialized with may feel uncomfortable inviting her out. She may be an unwelcome reminder of what could happen to any of them at any time, or as a single woman, she might be perceived as a threat to their marriages. Sheryl herself may feel like the third or fifth wheel in a social gathering of couples and choose not to attend. She may find the reminder of what she had lost too painful, leaving her without friends when she needs social support. If their friends were through Brian's place of work, she will no longer have that network to rely on. She may struggle to find new friends while grieving the loss of her husband.

For younger couples with children at home, if one spouse dies, there is the loss of the person who helped with the day-to-day responsibilities for raising those children. Now there is no one to help with getting children dressed and ready for school each day, or to pack lunches, or to take children to doctor or dentist appointments or attend parent-teacher conferences. The bereaved will need to take on these new tasks while dealing with their grief.

While there are commonalities that all those who face such losses experience, the loss of a spouse will affect the remaining spouse in differing ways depending on the unique relationship they had.

Loss of a Parent

Brian's children lost their father and all that entails for them. While adult children may no longer be living under the same roof and financially dependent on their parent, they might be dependent in other ways. Their parent may have been a friend and a trusted advisor. They will miss the role their parent played in their lives. They may realize that they are one step closer to death themselves. As long as both parents are alive, they stand as a barrier between them and death. When both die, not only is the barrier gone, they realize that they are orphans.

Young children who lose a parent will grow up with the grief. They might be preparing to graduate from high school and find themselves tearful as they think, "I wish my mom were here," or "I wish Dad were here." When they marry, amidst the joy of the celebration, there may be tears as they think how much their mom would have wanted to be here or a daughter may be wishing her dad were there to walk her down the aisle. They also struggle with feeling different from the other children in school. While the last thing that most teenagers want is to be like everyone else, they also struggle with not wanting to be too different and feeling alone in their loss. If the parent is the same sex, they have lost an important role model. If the opposite sex, they may struggle knowing how to relate to members of the opposite sex. If the remaining spouse is overcome by grief to the point of neglecting their children, the children will have lost not just one parent, but both. (More information on how children grieve is included in chapter 7.)

Loss of a Sibling

Brian's sister can't believe he is gone. The person she had fought with throughout her growing years, the person she had counted on to help her out of jams that she never told her parents about, the person who shared her memories of growing up in their parents' household. All of that is gone in one fell swoop now that he is gone. She didn't realize how much she relied on him until he was gone. And now there is no one else to help her take care of their mother. She is left alone, the sole remaining child.

No one knows us like our siblings. No one shares the same memories of growing up as our sibling. Often the loss of a sibling is discounted as not as important as the loss of a parent or child, but it is a significant loss, especially depending on the relationship. With their passing, death is that much closer as you realize, if it can happen to your brother or sister, it could happen to you.

In the case of young children, the remaining child may feel they need to take on traits of the sibling that died, or try to make it up to their parents for this loss. If their sibling died after a long illness, they may have felt neglected and been resentful of their sibling's need for care. They may feel guilty about this. As with all losses as a child, this loss will follow them as they grow up. As an adult they miss the relationship they were never able to have with their sibling, or may feel responsible in some way for their sibling's death. (more on this in the chapter on children and grief)

Parents who lose a child

Brian's mother, Betty, is lost without her son. He was her mainstay, providing help with handling her finances as well as help with repairs around the house. He had helped fill the void after her husband's death ten years earlier. What would she do now that he was gone? Why didn't she die instead? It was not right for a son to die before his mother. Who would take care of her now that he was gone?

No matter how old we are, we are still our parents' child. Betty still feels the loss of her child. Parents are not supposed to outlive their children. It upsets the natural order of life. Brian's mother is grieving but most of the support centers on Brian's wife, Sheryl. There isn't the same support available to parents of adult children as to parents of young children. Betty may be comforted by knowing Brian had lived a good and long life, but that still doesn't take away the pain of loss.

Another concern may be her relationship with Brian's wife and children. Fortunately, she had a good relationship with Sheryl and Brian's grown children. That isn't always the case. If the relationship between them and their in-laws is troubled, grandparents may lose not only their child but their grandchildren. This is not as much of an issue with grown grandchildren who likely have their own relationship with their grandparents, but can be especially problematic with young children if the remaining spouse chooses not to keep in contact with their deceased spouse's parents. The parent then experiences the loss not only of her child, but the child's children.

In the case of young children, grandparents can help fill some of the roles left empty by the loss of their child, perhaps filling in as a babysitter after their grandchildren get home from school or taking children to after-school activities or doctor appointments, or cooking a meal once a week. This requires that the grandparent work with the remaining parent in a way that is supportive of that parent and beneficial to both.

The Loss of a Young Child

Couples that lose a young child experience great stress to their marriage, one of the greatest stressors a marriage may endure. While some may be torn apart by the loss and end in divorce, thereby multiplying their losses, others are able to pull together and find ways to support each other in their loss. If the death were the result of an accident, parents may blame themselves or their spouse as they struggle to make sense of the loss. If after a prolonged illness, there may have been substantial financial burdens placed on the family and years of stress related to their child's care. In both situations parents are likely to feel like failures in this very important life role. They have failed to protect their child. If there are other children in the family, those children may have been neglected as their parents focused on their sibling. Anger and blame are common along with sorrow. Not only have they lost their child, they have lost their stake in the future, someone to carry on the family name, their legacy, all of the hopes and dreams associated with that child.

They may experience survivor guilt that they lived when their child didn't. If the death were from a car accident and they were in the car with their child, the guilt is multiplied. They may ask, why my child? Why not me? They may blame themselves for the accident, asking, why hadn't they left their child at home? They may feel guilt for not having protected their child. Anger may be manifested at God for taking their child from them. If another driver was at fault, anger will be directed at the driver. They may seek retribution through a court case. If their child was the victim of violence, their grieving will be complicated by the legal system as they wait for justice.

In their grief it is important that the siblings of their child are not forgotten. They are grieving too and need support. Sometimes after the loss of one child, parents may become over-protective and overly concerned about the remaining children out of fear of losing them too. Or they may look to their other children to take on roles fulfilled by their deceased child. In some cases, couples may have another child as a replacement child. This is detrimental to their other children. Parents may not recognize what they are doing, so they may need help to become aware of this dynamic.

Grandparents may also be forgotten during this time as their loss is considered to be less than the parents. Not only will they grieve the loss of their grandchild, they will worry about their adult child, how they are coping. If their adult child turns away from them in their grief, they may feel that they have lost their child as well as their grandchild.

While the intensity of the grief will lessen over time, the grief will follow them throughout their life and surface at different times. The parents may find themselves thinking, "Suzie would have been five this year," or "This is the year Tommy would have graduated from high school." When their other children reach milestones, they will celebrate these milestones, but may find moments of sadness as they remember the child who will never reach that milestone.

Miscarriage

In situations of miscarriage, the parents will experience the same grief from losing a child without receiving the social support they need because the loss is not recognized. Others may not have been aware of the pregnancy, or if aware, the pain is considered to be less.

Parents often start forming dreams about children before they are conceived. Once they learn they are pregnant, those dreams become more real and they begin bonding with the child. They may grieve that they never had a chance to get to know this baby, never got to hold the child or see their face. If possible, depending on the gestational age, it can be helpful to the grieving process to have parents hold the miscarried fetus and find ways to memorialize the loss through prayer and ritual.

Most often miscarriages are because there was a problem with the baby that precluded bringing the child to full term. Parents may feel guilty that they did something to cause the miscarriage. Mothers may worry that there was something wrong with them that caused the miscarriage and wonder whether they will ever be able to carry a child full term. Reassuring her that she can have other children doesn't take away from the pain of this loss. If she does become pregnant again, she will worry until she gets past the time of the previous miscarriage. Both parents may try to withhold bonding with the baby until then out of fear of the pain if there is another miscarriage.

Stillbirth

In cases of stillbirth, the parents have longer to prepare emotionally for the arrival of the baby and bond with it. They may have a nursery set up at home, stocked with supplies and baby toys. These are painful reminders of what they have lost when they come home from the hospital without a baby.

There is more social support available to the couple as this loss is recognized as a death. The parents have the opportunity to name the baby and hold the baby before saying goodbye. Funeral services may be held where friends and family gather and support the grieving parents. Again there will be the loss of the hopes and dreams for this child and feelings of guilt and anger. Did I do something wrong? Is it me? Parents might ask. If they get pregnant again, they will worry about it happening again until they deliver a healthy baby.

SIDS – Sudden Infant Death Syndrome

All of the factors involved in the previous situations apply to death by SIDS, Sudden Infant Death Syndrome. Parents have more time to bond with their baby. SIDS deaths are complicated by the involvement of the legal system as police investigate the death. At a time when grieving the loss of their baby, parents have to deal with police investigations, some may even be charged with crimes. Since the cause of SIDS is not evident, an autopsy may be required. This can help parents with the grieving process if they find reasons why their child died, reasons that are not associated with anything wrong on their part. Otherwise they may continue to question and worry about any future children they may have.

Abortion

In the case of an abortion, the parents may feel all of the losses experienced by parents of miscarried babies, with added guilt that they had caused the loss of life. Or they may experience relief at first, only to be beset by grief later. While not everyone experiences guilt, enough parents encounter it to make it important that the loss be acknowledged and the mother given support. Sometimes this grief doesn't surface until years later. If they have difficulty conceiving a child when ready to have children, they may feel it is because of their earlier abortion. They may consider it a judgment against them for the abortion. They may hear about another mother's miscarriage and find themselves grieving out of proportion to the loss because it brings up unresolved grief and guilt from the abortion. Counseling may be necessary for them to process the feelings and find the ability to forgive themselves and move on with their life.

Children with disabilities

You are there in the delivery room, awaiting the birth of your child. The moment you've been waiting for, dreamed about, is finally here. Your child is delivered, but there is a problem. Not something anyone wants to hear. Perhaps the child has Down syndrome or a birth defect. You check for the ten fingers and ten toes, check to make sure all of the body parts are there and functioning. The perfect child you dreamed about is not perfect.

Again, you experience the loss of your dreams about this child, your vision of what you expected. All of your plans for their future have to be modified. Perhaps they will never walk. You will never be able to coach their Little League games, or go to their dance recitals. It is another form of death that needs to be grieved in order to accept the child that you do have and embrace that child.

Every child is unique, requiring us to let go of our own expectations and dreams for that child as they insist on being their own person, but this can be challenging for the parent of a child with a disability. Denying your grief that your child is not what you expected is not helpful. The grief needs to be worked through, same as any grief. Children with disabilities pose many challenges, but they may also bring unexpected joy, once the grief is worked through and the reality of the situation accepted.

Infertility

Infertility can feel like a death to couples experiencing it. It is the death of their dreams of having a child together. As such, it needs to be grieved and recognized as the loss it is before the couple is able to pursue other avenues for having children. You can always adopt, well-meaning friends may say. Or you can find other ways to nurture children, they may say. While this may be true, it is not helpful to those dealing with the pain of infertility. They need a chance to grieve their loss before embarking on a new life.

I had a dream Monday night that I was holding a baby boy - he was pink and chubby and so, so perfect. The prevailing feeling in this dream was an intense euphoria. There's really no other way I can explain it. It was just me sitting on my bed holding this baby. We were both kind of glowing and completely wrapped up in the perfection of the moment.

When I was waking, I fought to go back to sleep. It was one of those dreams that you never want to wake from. I've only had a few like that in my whole life.

Tomorrow it will be 14 years since we held our son, Joshua, as he slipped from his earthly life into eternity. I can't help but wonder if my dream was a subconscious recognition of my heart remembering. I used to get pretty sick every year around this time. Heartsick that sometimes became physically sick.

I have not experienced that this year. Just many thoughts about him - and this dream. The baby I held in this dream did not look like our tiny sickly babe. But I think it's another puzzle piece in the healing process. A heart deep knowing that what we see here is not the real deal. We're not home. Our realities lie in another place. - One mother's reflections on the loss of her baby

Chapter 7

Children and Grief

Brian's daughter Theresa glanced out the window of the funeral home at her children playing with their cousins. They seemed completely unaffected by the loss of their grandfather. She was glad for this. That night though, her five-year-old daughter climbed onto her lap and asked when Grandpa was coming back.

"He's not coming back," she told her.

"Not ever?"

"Not ever."

"That's a long time. I miss him."

"I miss him too." Theresa held her tight.

Children may at times give the impression that they are unaffected by a loss. One minute they may be happily playing with friends, another they are crying inconsolably. Some claim children do not grieve until they are able to understand death. Others point to evidence of grief in babies separated from their primary caretaker. Babies as early as six months may show signs of withdrawal and depression when they experience such a loss.

William Worden believes children do grieve, just in their own ways based on their ability to understand their loss. They grieve in age-appropriate ways that change as they grow and their reasoning abilities increase. A four-year-old may not be able to understand that death is permanent. They may perceive it as temporary. They will keep asking when the deceased is coming back, which can be upsetting to the adults around them as they have to keep repeating the same answers. Each time the child asks about the deceased loved one it brings back pain from the loss. It can be painful to have to keep reminding small children that Grandma or Grandpa is not coming back.

Pre-school aged children have a very limited understanding of death. They see it as temporary, much like the games of hide and seek they played as babies. They have learned that objects that they don't see are not gone (object permanency), part of Piaget's first stage of cognitive development, and so they think the loved one is gone but will come back. They also don't understand that death is inevitable.

They may engage in magical thinking. Children have so little power over their life. This can be frightening to them. We all like to feel we have some power and control over our lives. Children respond to this lack of control by magical thinking, giving themselves the illusion of control. Not so different from adults. We have more sophisticated means of maintaining our illusions of control, but they are still illusions. If a child was angry at their mom or dad and one or both parents die in a car crash, they may believe they caused the death. Maybe they were angry at a sibling and shouted that they hated them. If the sibling dies, they may feel it was because of them. This magical thinking needs to be recognized and addressed. They need to be reassured that they had nothing to do with the death.

They do not have the ability to think in abstract terms so they will think in terms of concrete images. Death to them may be a person or being, the grim reaper or some other ghostly image. They will need concrete explanations of how someone died. When talking to young children about death, it is important to use concrete terms. Without going into unnecessary details, let them know what caused a death.

"Grandma was very sick. That's why she died. But she lived a long life, a good life."

If you say Grandma went to sleep, they may be afraid to go to sleep for fear that they will not wake up. If you say Grandpa went away, they will wonder when Grandpa is coming back. If you say God or Jesus took their loved one, they may see God as a cruel being who takes away the people they love. Be prepared to repeat answers to the same questions as they struggle to understand their loss.

In grade school, children understand that death is permanent but they may see it as far away and something that can be avoided, not inevitable for them. Magical thinking can persist as long as the age of nine, creating guilt. They may think that as long as they live a good life, they may be spared death. The concept of not-existing is very hard for even adults, much more so for young children who may lay in bed imagining monsters under the bed or in the closet.

By the time they reach their early teens, most children will have a concept of death that recognizes its permanence and inevitability, but teens still have a tendency to see it as far away, something that won't happen to them at least not for a long time. They have a tendency to test death through risk-taking activity. The loss of a classmate at this age shakes this belief as they recognize that if it happened to that person, it could happen to them. They fight accepting this. In their existential struggle for a sense of identity, they can be fascinated with thoughts of death. While teens have the ability to understand abstract concepts, they still have limited life experience and are learning coping skills.

Children who lose a parent will worry about who will take care of them. As long as their needs are provided for and their lives not overly disrupted, they will manage. Children's ability to deal with loss is related to the remaining parent's ability to cope. If their parent sinks into a depression and is unable to care for their children, the children will be doubly affected. If their life is completely upset and overturned, say they are sent to live with grandparents in a new city, this compounds their losses. However if life remains relatively the same, they continue to live in the same house, go to the same school, are taken care of, the loss will be easier for them.

Help children deal with their grief by talking to them in age-appropriate ways. Don't go into details about the death, but do tell children enough so that they understand what happened and that they had nothing to do with the death. Allow them to grieve in their own way and own time. Sometimes children act out their grief in their play. They need time to play, to be children. Just because they don't give the appearance of grieving, that doesn't mean they are not experiencing any loss. They just express it differently from adults.

At the time of death, allow the children to be part of the funeral. Perhaps they can make a memory book of their parent. Drawing and coloring can help a child express their grief. Talk to the child when they want to talk. Don't avoid their questions.

The child will grow up with their grief. As they reach milestones, they will miss their parents. As they grow and their ability to understand their loss develops, grief may resurface. This is part of the healing process.

Chapter 8

The Elderly and Grief

At seventy-five, Brian's mother, Betty, has already experienced many losses in her life. She has lost her parents, her husband, a sibling and a number of friends. And now a son. By the time someone has reached their senior years, you would think they have had enough experience with death and loss to be better at handling it. That is not the case. Every loss is different. They may have more experience, but it is still not easy.

Sometimes it may seem that the losses pile up, one after another. They may experience a loss overload as members of their family die, leaving them the last living member of their generation. Friends pass on as well so that they have more friends in heaven than on earth. It can be a blessing to live a long life, but it is a mixed blessing as so many losses accumulate. Seniors may begin to question why God hasn't taken them yet.

Those dealing with dementia or Alzheimer's may forget that their loved ones are gone. This can cause pain when family or friends mention the loved one and the senior with dementia replies in shock as if this were their first time hearing this. For them it is the first time. In my years as chaplain at a retirement community, I learned to be careful when talking with seniors with dementia after one time expressing my sorrow for a loss only to have the woman respond in tears, "He's dead? I didn't know he was dead. When did he die?" Sometimes, family needs to be prepared to explain repeatedly that someone has died, other times it is best to go along with whatever their loved one believes.

Added to the loss of family and friends, are the other losses of aging, as one by one physical abilities may be taken away. The ability to see, the ability to hear, to walk freely, even memories and the ability to think and reason clearly may be taken away from them. Being able to communicate with others is our primary means of achieving social support. The loss of hearing in old age greatly impairs this ability to communicate, thereby lessening their means of social support. As seniors age, they may become unable to live in their homes, requiring a move into a retirement community or a child's home. Another loss. There is the loss of freedom if they are no longer able to drive a car. There is also a loss of employment as they retire from work that gave meaning to their life.

In cases of retirement, it helps to have something in place to help replace all that was lost. For some people, a job is just a job, but for others it can be an important part of their identity and provide a sense of self-worth. The loss of such a position can result in a struggle to redefine oneself as someone beyond what they did. They can feel they no longer have any worth in the eyes of the world, and in their own eyes. They may need to grieve this loss of identity and find new ways to feel accomplishments and self-worth.

Retirement can be a wonderful time to do all the activities they never had time to do while working. It can be a time of rebirth and new life. Or it can be a time of feeling out of place and out of sorts.

As seniors go back over all they lost and share these memories, tears may surface, but that is okay. They need those tears. They need those memories. Some may say not to encourage Grandma or Grandpa in speaking about memories that bring them pain out of their own discomfort with grief. As in other situations of grief, you don't want to leave someone in their pain, but you don't want to avoid it. Use "dosing" (chapter 3) – a mixture of sad memories and distraction from that sadness. Some days they may need to be sad as they reminisce, others they may need diversions from the sadness. Let them visit the past, but not live there.

When she was eight years old, her stepmother became very ill, and she still remembered vividly her father's hoarse voice call from her stepmother's bedside, "She's gone." As the woman shared these memories, tears welled up in her eyes, and she began to cry. We were all silent, realizing how present that moment from eighty years past was to her. Then I said to her, "Those are painful memories." She stopped crying, looked up, and almost defiantly replied: "Those are sacred memories." The woman next to her added, "They are holy memories. We need such memories." (Fischer, p. 46)

Reminiscing, remembering and trying to make sense of their life are important parts of aging. Friends and family can support seniors in this by listening to their stories, helping them find themes and meaning in the story. Sometimes it's enough to just listen.

Chapter 9

Other Losses

Divorce

Divorce is the death of a marriage. Divorced individuals experience all of the loss that the bereaved spouse does with some differences. Some claim that it is a harder loss than an actual death. If you lose a spouse through death, at least you have your memories of the love you had. With divorce the love has died, leaving the newly divorced wondering, where did it go? What happened? Was it real?

This applies equally to men and women. Statistically, women apply for divorce more often than men. However, regardless of who initiates the divorce, their spouse is often left in a state of shock, especially if they had been unaware of their spouse's unhappiness. The one left behind questions, is it too late? Isn't there something I can do, we can do? Not realizing that their spouse may have been thinking about this for a long time before taking action.

Another problem area is determining when it is over. Divorced individuals may struggle with the first task – accepting the reality of the loss. They may hold out hope that they will get back together again. They may have a hard time accepting that the marriage truly is over. Even after the divorce papers are signed and filed in court, they may still be thinking it isn't real. He or she will come back to me.

They may need help accepting the reality. Sometimes it can be helpful to ritualize the loss. Wedding rings are a powerful symbol of the marriage. Some people bury their wedding ring to symbolize the death of the marriage. A gathering with friends to mourn the loss or celebrate the new life and the freedom of being single may be helpful as well.

Someone who initiates the divorce may focus on the negatives in the relationship, not acknowledging any positive aspects of the marriage or recognizing any need to grieve. They may need help doing this by reminding them of the good aspects of the relationship that they lost. Not only have they lost the relationship, they have lost all of the time they had invested into the relationship, all of the memories they shared, good and bad. While those memories remain, the one person they would have shared them with is no longer available. They have lost their dreams about having a marriage that lasts a lifetime and if children are involved, they may lose the role of full-time parent depending on how custody is set up.

I don't know of anybody who goes into a marriage planning for it to end. We go into marriage with so many hopes and dreams for the future. Those are all gone.

If there are children, they will grieve over the loss of their parents' marriage. There is no longer the same stigma associated with divorce as there was fifty years ago. Children no longer feel like they are the only ones that this has happened to, but they still grieve. They may hold onto the hope that their parents will remarry for years, even when their mom or dad is dating someone else. They might resist any attempt to bring a step-parent into the family because of this hope.

Sometimes parents can be so caught up in their own grief that they don't acknowledge their children's grief. Or the parent who initiated the divorce may ignore how it is affecting his/her children because they do not want to feel guilt over this. Parents need to put their own wounds aside in order to help their children. This includes not speaking ill of their former spouse in front of the children and seeking out ways to parent together despite the divorce.

It takes two people to make a marriage, but only one to end it. If your spouse decides he or she wants out of the relationship, there isn't anything you can do about it. The person who didn't initiate the divorce but was on the receiving end, may focus on what they lost, holding onto the disbelief that this is happening and holding onto the hope that their former spouse will return. They may need help moving on. You can help them see the problems in the marriage, acknowledge those problems, and choose to move on, learning from their previous problems in their marriage.

The person who initiated the divorce may have difficulty acknowledging the positives in the relationship for to do so may lead them to question their decision. Had they been right in seeking a divorce? Could they have tried harder?

As in loss through death, it doesn't help to idealize or demonize your partner. It does help to view the relationship as it was in all of its messiness, challenges and blessings.

Also as with death of a spouse, it can be tempting to form a new relationship before adequately grieving the first relationship. Many individuals do this only to find themselves replaying the same issues from the first relationship in the new relationship, because they haven't adequately completed the four tasks of grieving. When one part of the couple appears to be moving on and happy, the other may start to have regrets and rethink the divorce. Or seeing their former spouse happy in a new relationship may be what they need to finally accept that their marriage is over.

If you are open to it, you may discover that the divorce happened at just the right time. Maybe you didn't choose it, but you were ready to handle it. Longer and you may have stayed too long. Sooner and you would not have been ready.

Suicide

"I believe that the person who commits suicide puts his psychological skeletons in the survivor's emotional closet." Edwin Shneidman

I can't believe that she did this to us. Didn't he know how much it would hurt us? Hurt our children? Didn't she understand what her loss would do to us? Didn't he realize how much we loved him? These are just some of the questions that run through the heads of someone who loses a loved one through suicide. As mentioned in the quote above, they leave their skeletons in the survivors' closet, leaving them with a legacy of hurt, guilt and anger.

Survivors will be racked with guilt. They may wonder why they didn't see it coming, or if they were aware that something was wrong, they may feel guilty about not being able to help. They wonder, wasn't my love enough? Didn't he/she love me? He must not have loved me to do this. They may ask, doesn't he or she realize what this would do to those around them? The reality is that they were in so much pain that they couldn't see beyond the pain to how it would affect those they loved. Or even if they did recognize this, their own pain was so great they simply saw no other way out.

Suicide is a complicated act. It isn't always clear why someone would chose to take their own life or what constitutes a suicidal act. The person driving late at night who crashes into a tree and dies, was it an accident or a purposeful act to end their life? The alcoholic or drug addict who continues to use even though they are on a course likely to end their life. Or the anorexic or bulimic individual, intent on losing weight to the point of starving themselves to death. Was it a cry for help, as in some suicide attempts, or a determined, thought-out action? And what of those who give their life for others, are they acts of heroism or suicides?

The feelings associated with a suicide are strong: intense anger, sorrow, guilt. "If he were alive, I would kill him!" remaining friends and family may say. Complicating the grieving process can be the tendency for the loss to have a stigma associated with it. While this has changed substantially over the years, there are still those who view suicide as socially unacceptable, thereby robbing the bereaved of necessary social support.

Some family members may worry about other family members after a suicide being prone to suicide. Once the social strictures against taking your own life has been breached, it can appear more possible. This can account for the occurrence of copycat suicides in high schools where one student suicide is followed by others. Once the unspeakable happens, it becomes a possible solution to problems.

There are cases where suicides may run in a family. A genogram may show a history of suicides. It is not hereditary, but having had a family member complete suicide can put a person at a greater risk. Sons of fathers who completed suicide are particularly vulnerable. They need to be reassured that this does not have to be the case. There is no genetic basis for this, but there could be a social basis because of the family history. Knowing this can help children be aware of the possibility and do what is necessary to prevent a recurrence of the pattern. They may find themselves struggling as they approach the age of the parent who completed suicide.

Humans crave wholeness. The path to wholeness is often through our past hurts and losses. As they approach the age of the parent, this may open the door to greater understanding of their deceased parent and why they may have chosen to take this path, leading to healing. Healing from the loss of a loved one is never completely done. Memories and sadness will resurface through our lives, a reminder of what we have lost. But it does get better.

When dealing with situations of suicide, treat it as you would any other death. Go to the visitation and funeral. Talk about the one who died, share memories with the family. They will appreciate them. Don't be afraid to mention the suicide. This lets family members know that you are aware of what they are dealing with, that they are not alone, that what their loved one did was not unspeakable.

Loss of Employment

The loss of a job is another form of dying. Gone are the plans you may have had, gone is the structure to your day that a job provides, the meaning it provided, as well as the financial stability. Suddenly you may be forced to look for new employment in order to provide for yourself and your family. There may not be time to grieve the loss of the position as you seek out new work. Gone are the networks of friends you have at work.

Even if you chose to quit, there is still loss. With every life change or transition, there are losses to grieve, even as you take on a new adventure. If moving from one position to another without a break in between, you will be grieving the one loss while embarking on new beginnings. This can complicate the new beginnings. You feel sad even though happy about the new position. Those who quit may downplay the losses, focusing on why they wanted to leave, while those fired may focus on the good aspects of the position, downplaying the negatives.

In the introduction, you saw two different ways to lose employment. The grief involved was different because of how each was handled. The loss experienced at the end of employment will be as different as the people involved and the circumstances around the loss.

As in divorce, if you are open to it, you may discover that the loss of employment happened at just the right time. Maybe you didn't choose it, but you were ready to handle it.

Loss of a pet

During high school, my daughter spent two weeks in a village in Mali as part of Building with Books. While there, whenever she saw a dog and asked its name, the response was always the same, the Mali word for dog. Clearly their relationship with dogs is different from our relationships with our pets here in America. In a society where they struggled to provide for the needs of their children, there were no resources to invest in pets.

When we were a rural, agrarian society, animals were valued more for their function. Horses provided a means of transportation or for hauling goods. Farm animals were a source of food. Dogs served a function as well, perhaps herding sheep or protecting chickens or family members. Cats caught mice that might steal food from the family or get into grain bins. Their role as companion was not their primary role as it is today.

Now in America, pets are part of the family, especially our dogs and cats. We name them, buy treats for them, take them to the vet, dress them up and buy them Christmas gifts. As part of the family, their loss is grieved.

We invest meaning into our pets. They may fill a void in our life, or a need. Depending on the need they fill, our grief at their loss will be greater or lesser.

When my mother lost her dog forty years ago, she was inconsolable. At the same time, she had been going through empty nest syndrome as the youngest of my siblings had gone off to college. She had fussed over that dog, lavishing care on it as if it were a baby. She let it sit in her lap at the dinner table and fed it treats. That dog was more than a pet to her. It was someone to take care of now that her children were gone. It was filling a need for her at that time. She had other dogs after that one but she didn't mourn their loss as much as she did this one.

In grieving the loss, it is important to recognize the role the pet played in that individual's life. Perhaps the dog was a child's primary source of comfort during a parent's illness and death. Losing that pet will bring back that loss as well as the pain from the loss of the pet. Perhaps the pets served as surrogate children for a childless couple. Their loss will be grieved more because of what the pet represented.

Pets, especially dogs, provide unconditional love. They greet you at the door with their tail wagging and don't hold grudges against you. (Their memory span is limited so they forgive easily!) A family pet may hold different meanings to the different members of the family. Some may experience more grief at the death of a pet than the death of a family member, depending on the role the pet played in the person's life and the relationship with the family member. The pet owner may feel guilty about this.

It's important to acknowledge the loss. My vet sends sympathy cards when a pet dies, a simple acknowledgment that a loss has happened and the grief that evokes. For children, the loss of a pet may be their first experience with death and needs to be addressed to help prepare for future losses.

Loss of a Limb – Amputation

Many liken the loss of a loved one to an amputation. A part of them has been ripped off. They feel phantom pain long after the loss. This can be a helpful metaphor.

The actual loss of a limb is a death experience. Life as you know it will never be the same. While you can still have a quality life, it is different. Besides the actual physical pain associated with the loss, there is the pain from losing your ability to do what you once did. If the loss of a leg, you will no longer be able to walk freely. While prosthetics are improving daily, allowing people to move about freely again, the leg will have to heal from the amputation first and then it will take some time of adjustment. As with other losses, there is so much you take for granted until it is gone. You may not recognize the full extent of your loss at first. If you lose your left arm and you are right-handed, you still use the left hand for so many things including balance and lifting. The adjustment may be easier than with the loss of your dominate hand, but it will be a significant adjustment none-the-less.

The loss of good health, being diagnosed with a chronic or life threatening illness, will also bring their share of grief. You will need to recognize and grieve your losses before going on to your new life, embracing what you have left.

Loss of a Home

The loss or destruction of a home through a fire, flood, or other disaster, is much more devastating than the loss of a home through a move. In the destruction of your home, you may lose many precious articles that make a house a home: pictures of family members, keepsakes, gifts from loved ones, items that cannot be replaced. There can be a sense of violation when your home is destroyed, but as with all losses, it can be also be an opportunity to reflect on what is most important. One woman remembered the months living in a trailer with her family while their home was rebuilt after a fire as some of the best months of their life together. She remembered the hours she had spent before the fire organizing favorite recipes that were then lost, as time that could have been better spent elsewhere. All they had lost had been material items. What was important was that none of them had been hurt.

In a move, all of those precious items move with you to your new home, making it easier. You may grieve certain aspects of your old home that may not be in your new home: the wrap-around front porch with a swing, space for a garden, a walk-in closet. You may also miss the memories associated with that particular space. While you carry your memories with you, there is something about how visiting physical locations will wake up forgotten memories.

There is so much involved with moving from one place to another. As with other losses, we rarely realize the extent of our loss until afterwards. If moving from one city to another city, there are more losses than those involved with moving from one home to another within a close geographical location. If the move is not far, you don't lose all of the friendships and connections you have, though you most likely lose neighbors you may have come to know.

When moving greater distances, you lose all of the relationships you have developed over time in that area. Yes, thanks to modern technology, it is easier to keep in contact with friends through the internet and social media; still, it is harder to meet up for coffee or drinks at your favorite location. You lose the ease of getting around from one place to another as you learn your way around. And you lose all those favorite spots, such as the convenient coffee place a block away from your home or on your way to work. Or your favorite take-out or pizza joint. You may be surprised at what you miss the most. When I moved to north Flint, Michigan, from Lansing many years ago, I was unable to find a good pizza place. I tried out a number of locations and was disappointed so that I eventually gave up.

You will need to find new places to shop. Your favorite grocery store may be non-existent in your new locale, forcing you to try new ones. You may feel disoriented for a number of months as you find your way. If you move from a large city to a country area, you may grieve the loss of the activity and excitement that the city offered. If from the country to the city, you may grieve the loss of quiet and be upset by all of the people and traffic. You may find yourself grieving over what you lost, even after a well thought out move.

Allow yourself to grieve your losses even as you embrace your new life. Eventually all that is new and confusing will become familiar.

Chapter 10

General Principles to Help Families

Besides the specific ways to help listed in each chapter on the four tasks of mourning, there are some general principles to follow in regards to your own grief and the grief of others.

1. Assist in moving through the four tasks.

Wherever they are in regards to the tasks, meet them there and help them move on to the next. Wherever you are, start there. Perhaps you are still struggling to admit the loss really happened. Talk about the death and the funeral to help you acknowledge this. Perhaps you are overwhelmed with feelings. Allow the feelings to come to the surface, then let them go. Perhaps you are struggling with all of the little things your loved one did now that they are no longer around to do them. Make a list and figure out what needs to be done, when and by whom. Or if you are having a hard time embracing what is left of your life and making new beginnings, start small and allow yourself to feel good about yourself and your life. Remember the tasks are not to be maneuvered in lock-step, but can be done simultaneously or may require going back to an earlier task.

2. Don't impose a time line for others or yourself.

Much as people may want to have a time line, don't set one. You can give general guidelines, such as, you may tell them that many people take a year or more after a major loss to start to feel like they are moving on. But remind them that it takes as long as it takes. There are no firm rules in place. Everybody grieves at their own pace and in their own way. Give yourself and others the freedom to set that pace.

3. Don't judge yourself or others.

Don't impose "shoulds" or "shouldn'ts", especially in regards to feelings. Just because someone is not visibly grieving a loss, that doesn't mean they aren't. They just may be expressing their grief differently. Worden tells of a wife and daughter who were convinced their husband/father was not allowing himself to grieve. The man, a farmer, spent his days on his tractor. When Worden spoke to him, he acknowledged that this was how he grieved his loss. There is no right or wrong way to grieve a loss, just some guidelines. Don't be judgmental of someone who doesn't follow your way of grieving.

4. Deal with unfinished business.

Often after a death, we may feel we have unfinished business, things we never said or did that now we can't say or do. One way to help with unfinished business is to write a letter to the deceased loved one. In it you can express everything you were never able to say to your loved one while alive. Another way is to go to the gravesite and speak to your loved one. Or simply tell another person what you wanted to say to your loved one. Counselors may use the empty-chair technique to help with this where they tell the bereaved to imagine that their loved one is sitting in an empty chair and encourage them to carry on a conversation with them. They say what they want to say, then imagine what they think their loved one would say in response, with assistance from the counselor. Another use of the empty chair is to have the bereaved sit in the chair after they have spoken to their loved one and imagine what the deceased would say if they were present.

5. Use journals.

Journals are a great way to express feelings, memories, hopes and dreams. Journal writing can be very healing for the bereaved. In the journal they can express any and all feelings without being judged. They can vent their anger at their loved one, at God, at the world, ask questions, share memories, write about hopes and dreams for the future that have been dashed by the person's death and seek out new dreams. Write without worrying about spelling, grammar, or sentence structure. Just allow the words to flow. The exercise is not for publication but for healing.

6. Recognize other losses.

As you deal with one loss, other losses may surface from your past. In some cases it may be because they have yet to be resolved, or it may be that they were resolved in the past, but now other issues have come to the surface that you weren't aware of back then. Deal with these losses the same as you are dealing with the new loss. Also look for concurrent losses, losses that arise from the loss, and address these as well.

7. Seek out the support you need.

Whether through friends, family, church, grief support groups or other social networks, look for the support you need to get through this. Don't be afraid to ask for what you need. If you can't get this through your circle of friends and family, look for other avenues for support. If you feel you are stuck, seek out professional help through a grief counselor.

8. Be gentle with yourself and others.

Grieving is work. It can be extremely difficult and emotionally demanding. As such it can drain your energy. You may feel like you are not accomplishing anything. You are accomplishing something – the important job of healing. You don't expect someone with a broken bone to be healed in three days, and yet we expect that of ourselves when it comes to the loss of a loved one. As mentioned in chapter one, the loss of a loved one can be as psychologically traumatic as experiencing physical trauma such as severe burns. Be sure to take care of yourself as you deal with this trauma. You have survived another day without your loved one. Some days will be harder than others but with the passage of every day, it will get better.

Chapter 11

Conclusion – The Promise of a New Day

Grieving is a slow process. It can't be rushed through for it takes as long as it takes; it is a part of life. As C.S. Lewis tells us, "The sorrow now is part of the happiness then. That's the deal." Or as the poet Michael Lynch says, "Grief is the tax you pay on love." It is the price we pay for having loved another. The only way to avoid grief is to be detached and not allow ourselves to love, to go through life only half alive, not a choice many make. As such, grief is a gift, one we don't want, but a gift none-the-less. We need to know how to unwrap it.

At the end of the road, there is hope. We can get through this. We may go through times of despair and darkness where it feels there is no light ahead of us, only more darkness. But as we go through each day, there is the promise of new life and new beginnings, and we are never left alone in our struggles. Our God is present, even when we don't feel God's presence. There are others who have walked the same path before us, and friends and family walking with us in this journey.

Our life will be better, richer, from what we have suffered, for it means we have loved much.

Acknowledgments

It may be spring outside, yet inside its winter when you are experiencing grief. Under the snow lies new life, if we can but get there. But sometimes it seems we will never experience joy again.

In my 35 years of ministry, I've been privileged to walk with many individuals through loss, as well as encountered my own losses. I've also taught courses on Grief Counseling. This book is the fruit of those years of experience. Thank you to the people who have allowed me into their life, and to those who have walked alongside me during my own times of grief. I couldn't have done it without you.

SELECTED RESOURCES

Canine, J. (1996). *The psychosocial aspects of death and dying.* New York: McGraw Hill.

DeSpelder, L.A. & Strickland, A.L. (2011). *The last dance: Encountering death and dying*. Ninth Edition. New York: McGraw Hill.

Fischer, K (1998). *Winter grace: Spirituality and aging*. Nashville, TN: Upper Room Books.

L'Engle, M. (1988). *Two Part Invention: The Story of a Marriage.* San Francisco: Harper & Row Publishers.

Lewis, C.S. (1961). *A grief observed*. San Francisco, CA: Harper Collins.

Moyers, B. (1999). *On our own terms, Moyers on dying* (DVD). Athena.

Rando, T. (1984). *Grief, dying and death: Clinical interventions for caregivers.* Champagne, IL: Research Press.

Walsh-Burke, K. (2006). *Grief and loss: Theories and skills for helping professionals.* Pearson Education, Inc.

Worden, W.J. (2009). *Grief counseling and grief therapy.* Fourth Edition. New York: Springer Publishing Co.

Wright, H.W. (2004) *Experiencing grief.* Nashville, TN: Broadman & Holmann Publishers.

Other Non-Fiction Books by Patricia Robertson

Daily Meditations (with Scripture) for Busy Moms, ACTA Publications.

From I Do to We Do: The First Five Years. Dreamweaver Press.

Marriage Moments I & II, Marriage Matters Jackson.

They Do Grow Up: Parents and Teens Talk, Liguori Publications.

The Rosary: Worry Beads for Anxious Parents, St. Anthony Messenger Press.

Walking with Families through the Dying Process. Dreamweaver Press.

Who Me? Full of Grace? Spirituality for Moms. Dreamweaver Press.

Plus numerous fiction books. For more information go to www.patriciamrobertson.com.

ABOUT THE AUTHOR

Patricia M. Robertson is an author, speaker and spiritual director, who is committed to helping individuals find God in their everyday experience. Married, mother and minister, she writes for and about ordinary people living extraordinary lives just by being the person they are meant to be with all their human failings and foibles.

Patricia has Doctor of Ministry degree and over thirty-five years of ministry experience. During this time she has walked with many families through the experience of death and loss.

She is a published author of fiction and non-fiction books, including a companion to this book, *Walking with Families through the Dying Process.* She blogs through her website.

For more information go to her website, https://patriciamrobertson.com